Top Notes

Steven Herrick's

The Simple Gift

Study notes for Standard English:
Second edition
Module C 2015–2020 HSC

Clarissa Greenhalgh

A
FIVE SENSES
PUBLICATION

Five Senses Education Pty Ltd
2/195 Prospect Highway
Seven Hills 2147
New South Wales
Australia

Greenhalgh, Clarissa
Top Notes – The Simple Gift
ISBN 978-1-76032-050-8

CONTENTS

INTRODUCTION TO THE TOP NOTES SERIES

This series has been created to assist HSC students of English in their understanding of set texts. Top Notes are easy to read and provide analysis of issues and discussion of important ideas contained in the texts.

Particular care has been taken to ensure that students are able to examine each text in the context of the module and specific elective to which it has been allocated.

Each text includes:

- Notes on the specific module
- Plot summary
- Character analysis
- Setting
- Thematic concerns
- Language studies
- Essay questions and a response
- Other textual material if required
- Additional questions
- Useful quotes

I am sure you will find these Top Notes useful in your studies of English.

Bruce Pattinson
Series Editor

THE STANDARD COURSE

This is a brief analysis of the Standard course to ensure you are completely familiar with what you are attempting in the examination. If in any doubt at all, check with your teacher or the Board of Studies.

The Standard Course requires you to have studied:

- Four prescribed texts. This means four texts from the list compiled by the Board of Studies.
- For each of the texts, **one** must come from **each** of the following four categories.
    - drama
    - poetry
    - prose fiction (novel usually)
    - non-fiction or media or film or multimedia texts. (Multimedia are CD ROMs, websites, etc.)
- A range of related texts of your own choosing. These are part of your Area of Study, Module A and Module C. Do not confuse these with the main set text you are studying.

Area of Study: Discovery

Module A	*Module B*	*Module C*
Experience through Language	**Close Study of Text**	**Texts and Society**
Electives	▪ Drama	*Electives*
▪ Distinctive Voices	OR	▪ Exploring Interactions
OR	▪ Prose Fiction	OR
▪ Distinctively Visual	OR	▪ Exploring Transitions
	▪ Nonfiction, Film, Media, Multimedia	
	OR	
	▪ Poetry	

You must study the Area of Study and EACH of Modules A, B and C

There are options within EACH of these that your school will select.

TEXTS AND SOCIETY

ELECTIVE TWO: Exploring Transitions

The Texts and Society module, Module C, requires an examination and analysis of texts which arise from or represent a particular situation or context. The syllabus states that,

> Modules...emphasise particular aspects of shaping meaning and representation, questions of textual integrity, and ways in which texts are valued.[1]

The Module's focus, therefore, must be kept in mind and not just the elective, "Exploring Transitions", when studying *The Simple Gift*. The idea of transition or movement resulting in change should be explored in and through the text. The Board of Studies directs students to,

> explore and analyse a variety of texts that portray the ways in which individuals experience transitions into new phases of life and social contexts[2].

Such explorations can be undertaken thematically, with a focus on the characters of Billy and Old Bill in particular and with reference to techniques and context.

Transitions should also be explored through the textual form, in this case, Herrick's choice of a verse novel. In this way the Module's mention of "Text" assumes significance and techniques assume importance. This focus on textual form and techniques applies not only your prescribed text, but also your related text

---

1   http://www.boardofstudies.nsw.edu.au/syllabus_hsc/pdf_doc/english-prescriptions-2015-20.pdf
2   Board of Studies Op Cit

choices. Ask how the poetic, filmic, narrative or other specific techniques linked to the textual form of your related material, contribute to representing transition within the given text.

"Exploring Transition" will involve looking at the origins of, the nature of and the consequences of the transition. It will involve theme, characterisation, recognition of textual form, analysis of features and techniques of that textual form and discussion of how form and features contribute to and convey the concept of transition.

"Exploring Transition" in and through a text should also involve an examination of the impact of context and values. Through exploring the significance of the context of composition and reception, then and only then will you really engage with the requirements of Module C Texts and Society, Elective 2, and not just Elective 2. Through a focus on transitions as represented in Text and as related to and reflecting aspects of Society, you will better "explore" rather than just identify transitions in your texts.

In order to compose highly regarded responses, do not use a narrow thematic lens to explore this issue but ensure you take a wider view which focuses on the set question, incorporates discussion of textual form and related techniques as well as the significance of context and societal values. In so doing you will have really shown understanding of your text, your elective and your module.

It is dissatisfaction with family and school life and a need for greater fulfilment which prompts Billy to change towns. Caitlin questions the values of her own social class and Old Bill makes a transition from business man to hobo due to personal tragedy. Billy's friendship and acceptance of Old Bill and Old Bill's kindness to Billy enabled further transitions to occur in both their personal lives.

The module requires that you come to an understanding of the specific ways that texts communicate ideas, bodies of knowledge, attitudes and values which are characteristic of different areas of society. Electives in this module focus on a particular social context and texts have been selected which reflect the importance of context. You will study the values and ideas which are characteristic of this context. It will be useful for you to spend some time researching the context in which *The Simple Gift* was written, to help you understand the text more thoroughly. Class and societal values form a backdrop for this verse narrative. Attitudes shaped by social class and challenges to such attitudes based on values are key concerns of this prescribed text.

Characters in this text gain self-awareness and the confidence to make their own choices. All these social aspects are represented and reflected in aspects of the text. For example, the changing narrative perspective or persona's voice, the characterisation and growth or relationships and the linear structure are worth focussing on.

A solid understanding of textual features is crucial to success in English in the HSC. You must, however, do more than simply list features and techniques. You need to also explain how the features and techniques (such as poetic and narrative techniques) communicate or represent transitions.

You will be expected to select supplementary material that appropriately relates to your text, elective and module. This does not mean that you have to choose a text, which was written or produced at the same time as your prescribed text, or which deals with characters from the same social class. It does mean that your text will also reflect transitions or changes which result from or respond to societal values and attitudes. These may be seen through social class divisions and be reflected in societal institutions. Billy, Old Bill and Caitlin's transitions are characterised by their new found and increasing ability to have choices and to be able to make decisions regarding life's direction. Speech, actions and opinions reflect changed perceptions and values. The proof of transition lies in the choices made and the changes which become evident in the characters' lives. Consider the nature of the transition in the related texts you select and the textual proof of such transitions.

The syllabus also requires you to examine transitions in terms of their nature and consequences. The syllabus states, "transitions may be challenging, confronting, exciting or transformative". They can also be examined in terms of their effects, "and may result in growth, change and a range of consequences for the individual and others... new knowledge and ideas, shifts in attitudes and beliefs, and a deepened understanding of the self and others.."[3] It is worth exploring the origins, the nature and the consequences of Billy's, Caitlin's and Old Bill's change and the origin of, nature of and consequences of the transitions encountered in your related texts. In this way, the rubric can be used to scaffold an approach to studying the theme of transitions and their content in texts while focus on techniques can explore how such transitions are represented and conveyed. Effectively, the Module and Elective should be seen as closely interrelated, so consider them together. Remember also that every examination

---

3   ibid

© Five Senses Education Pty Ltd

question arises from the rubric and examiners will expect that you focus on text, Module and Elective.

"Exploring Transitions" refers to how people grow and move into new phases of their life. Growth can be automatic or prompted by a trigger. Do not forget to consider titles. *The Simple Gift* gives a clue that part of transitioning will be because of or involve, a gift. This operates on various levels. Consider friendship, love, trust and faith as intangible gifts and the house as a concrete gift.

You will need to differentiate how individuals experience this growth and change differently. Finally, using this information you will respond to and compose your own texts which highlight your understanding of embarking on, experiencing and evaluating transitions.

Use the terminology that the Board of Studies provides in the rubric for the module and elective in your own responses and compositions for both assessments and the HSC examination. Apply it to your texts and provide textual referencing to support your points. This lets your teacher and the examiners know that you are indeed focused, that you know and understand the requirements as well as your prescribed and related texts.

The following lists of synonyms and related phrases may be useful in your composing and responding.

Exploring

- Probing
- Analysing
- Investigating
- Seeking

Transitioning

- Evolving
- Blossoming
- Expanding

- Maturing
- Growing
- Changing

- Budding
- Dawning
- Unfolding

- Seeking to reach a new goal
- Developing

- Moving towards a new stage of life
- Segueing

- Emerging
- Passing
- Transiting

- Shifting

Educating

- Training
- Teaching
- Fostering
- Enabling

Attitudes and Beliefs

- Values
- Assumptions
- Bias

- Positions
- Perspectives
- Viewpoints

Experience which can be linked to Transition

- Adventure
- Affair
- Incident
- Event
- Encounter
- Episode
- Exploit
- Feat
- Perception
- Occurrence
- Confrontation
- Decision
- Ordeal
- Venture
- Trial
- Profile
- Rendezvous

Textual Features

The following techniques and features may be particularly relevant to representing the idea of transition in a text -

- Narrative perspective and voice
- Confessional tone
- Contrast and juxtaposition
- Binary opposites -For example, Negative and positive tone
- Linear structure
- Bildungsroman genre
- Soliloquy
- Costuming/Description

Textual Forms

These textual forms may be relevant to representing Transition. Be sure to look at textual form, techniques and context when discussing links to meaning.

- Personal account/ Memoir
- Personal narrative
- Biography
- Film
- Polyptych (panelled Art)
- Narrative
- Poetry
- Picture book

IN SUMMARY:

This module and elective requires you to do the following with the prescribed text, *The Simple Gift,* and related material:

■ Engage with and explore the prescribed text and other related texts.

■ Understand what the texts say about personal change or transition.

■ Analyse how different characters deal with change. Explore their transitions in these texts, the prompts for them and the effects of them.

■ Determine the belief systems and ideology held by society in the context of the play's setting, composition and reception.

■ Understand how the belief systems and ideologies are represented using dramatic techniques.

■ Respond to and compose your own texts that explore the specific situation of "Exploring Transitions" using various language features that explore transitional phases.

WHY STUDY POETRY?

Poetry is a part of life and is about life. It deals with all the emotions of life: love, death, nature, friendship, feelings of pain, anger, frustration - all the moods and ideas that are part of the human condition. Poetry appeals to our understanding through our imagination, making us see what the poet has seen, hear what the poet has heard and experience his feelings.

USEFUL LITERARY TERMS

Familiarity with the following terms of figurative language, poetic device and technique will enable you to convince your examiner that you have acquired the vocabulary necessary to discuss how the composer attempts to share his ideas through the use of his poetic craft.

Alliteration	repetition of initial consonant sounds close together – for a special/poetic sound effect/ emphasis.
Allusion	a reference to something from history, literature, religion that adds to its meaning.
Analysis	to examine closely, take apart for the purpose of greater understanding.
Assonance	Repetition of vowel sounds in words or lines close together.
Cliché	word or phrase which is very common and overused.

Climax	Where emotions/ideas reach their a peak (often the end of a poem).
Criticism	Evaluation of literature, finding strong points which support the meaning, looking at style and language use.
Dissonance	Harsh sounding words together for a special effect and emphasis.
Enjambment	run-on-lines, with no punctuation pauses, having effect on the sense of the lines in the poem.
Free verse	a disregard for traditional rhyme/rhythm rules.
Hyperbole	exaggeration for effect/emphasis (e.g. 'millionth person').
Imagery	figures of speech -metaphors, similes etc. that make word pictures, comparisons or contrasts, to aid understanding.
Irony	a reversal of expected ideas used to make an effect,to draw attention to a point.
Juxtaposition	two contrasting ideas close together for dramatic effect .
Lyric	a poem that expresses emotions and ideas.

Metaphor	a direct comparison between two things, referring to one in terms of another - without using 'like' or ' as'
Mood	overall emotional effect/feeling set in a line or stanza of a poem.
Motif	dominant theme/object that comes up several times in a poem or collection of poems.
Narrative	style of writing which relates a story.
Onomatopoeia	words that imitate sound being described, used for the sound effect and emphasis.
Paradox	a contradiction which actually is true.
Personification	to give human qualities to non-living things.
Realism	make vividly real by careful attention to detail
Satire	criticise by means of subtle ridicule, with comic effect.
Simile	comparison used to describe something more vividly, using 'like' or 'as', to get a certain meaning across.
Stanza	divisions within a poem, similar to paragraphs in prose.

Structure	the shape or form of a poem, the way it hangs together.
Style	interplay of structure/ language/ tone that supports the theme.
Symbol	an image that stands for a complex idea.
Theme	central message/meaning of a piece of writing.
Tone	overall attitude conveyed by the writing to the audience through the combination of subject, mood and style.
Transferred epithet	figurative language where an idea is passed from one thing onto another for dramatic immediacy.

WHY STUDY FICTION? – TECHNIQUES

Narratives teach us about others, ourselves and our place in the world. They can also provide an escape and take us to other worlds. The act of reading itself is a transition as it takes the reader on an imaginative journey to another place.

Unusually, apart from being a collection of poems, this text is also told in a narrative style. The QUP edition has described it as a "free verse novel." Written with little adherence to rhythm and rhyme, the poems are connected and tell the story of the transitioning of three individuals, Billy, Old Bill and Caitlin. When discussing form, do not simply discuss this as poetry or only as a novel. It is both. The poetry presents changing personas. At times the voice and focalisation belongs to Caitlin, at other times, Bill or Old Bill. Minor characters such as Ernie even have poems presented from their perspective. This changing narrative perspective enables events to be experienced from numerous viewpoints and thus, it is a stylistic technique which strengthening the readers' understanding of the characters and situations.

Plot, setting and characterisation are all important narrative techniques. Ensure you consider each of them and there is plenty of detail included in this book.

The plot can be analysed in terms of style and structure. Under style may come literary devices such as imagery. Language refers to the words of the text and it is here that the flow of the poetry and the different narrative perspectives might be discussed.

THEME

Theme is an important aspect of any literature. Try always to find the theme in a poem, in other words the *central thread that runs through the work* that gives it its unique meaning. Often the title is the key to its meaning, so look there first. The title of a poem, or story or film is not decided on a whim – the composer puts a great deal of thought into it, and thus, to appreciate the text the title, and any sub-title should be considered.

Remember that the poet is presenting his ideas, feelings and arguments about life as he sees it. The reader has to work these out, and different readers may come up with different interpretations. Reading poetry can become very subjective (personal), as the reader recognises feelings and sympathises with the ideas, but poetry appreciation should be underpinned at all times by the text itself.

Useful hints for studying the themes of a text:

- **Brainstorm**

Make a record of all of messages that you believe the text held for you. You may be able to group many of these ideas together. For instance, love, friendship and influence can all be seen as part of the theme of relationships.

- **Organise your ideas**

Mind-maps or flow-charts are effective strategies for organising your ideas and working out the connections between themes and sub-themes.

- **Identify HOW the theme is presented**

Identify the features of the text that the composer has used to explore the theme. Narrative style, characterization or particular events in the narrative may reveal this theme.

- **Evidence**

Find specific quotes and examples from the text to include in your discussion of theme.

> Important Note:
>
> You will be expected to demonstrate an understanding of the themes of your texts (*The Simple Gift* and your related text) in your extended response. Another way of asking you to discuss the theme of the text is to ask you to discuss its message or meaning. Numerous themes such as Death, Grief, Identity, Control, the Power of Friendship and Overcoming Adversity are all relevant to this text.

STYLE

Poetry is a particular and special literary art form, and it is the style of writing that makes it different from the prose of novels. The reader should pay attention to the method of writing because a good poet will be very deliberate about form. There are many formal poetic devices that have been used down the ages to express a poet's ideas and emotions (rhyme, rhythm, language, punctuation etc). Modern free verse is not as disciplined as, for instance, a sonnet by Shakespeare which was limited to fourteen lines and a distinct rhyme scheme.

However, that does not mean that there is no 'style' to the poetry. It just may not be obvious at first - but it needs to be found through close scrutiny. Refer to the literary terms provided and see what has been used and how the Herrick has used it to convey his themes. Look at the stanza divisions, note the punctuation, pick up the sound effects of alliteration and assonance. Also remember, that while it is written in verse, this text also tells a story and has narrative elements. It is a verse novel.

THE COMPOSER- STEVEN HERRICK

Steven Herrick was born in Brisbane, in 1958 where he grew up as the youngest of seven siblings. At school his favourite subject was soccer and after he left school, at age fifteen, he continued to dream of football glory while he worked at a variety of odd jobs in factories and fruit picking. Faced with the reality, at eighteen, that he could not pursue a career in football and well aware that he did not want to work in factories for the rest of his life, Herrick wrote and published his first poem:

I had nothing to do one night and thought I'd write a poem...
some of my friends were in a rock band and I couldn't do that so I
thought I'd try and do something creative. I couldn't sing or play
guitar or anything like that so I tried pen and paper.

This poem was called 'Love is like a Gobstopper' and it earned him five dollars.

Herrick published his first book for adults, an anthology of poetry titled *Caboolture*, in 1988. His first book for children, *Water Bombs*, was published in 1992. Now, Steven Herrick writes for children and teenagers. He lives in the Blue Mountains with his wife and two sons and travels around Australia and overseas in order to perform his poems and talk to young people – in schools, universities, festivals, rock venues and on radio and television.

Steven Herrick draws inspiration for his writing from talking to young people about their lives and the way they see the world. He says:

I regard it my duty as a writer to represent children and teenagers
fairly.

In particular, he aims to celebrate the sense of humour and optimism he has observed amongst young people:

I am interested in showing how positive young people are.

Although the issues dealt with by Herrick including death and grief, self-image, belonging and homelessness, and how they impact on young people are serious, he chooses to explore them from a positive perspective. The characters we meet in Herrick's texts are generally good-hearted, they want to do the right thing, although their circumstances are often less than ideal. The main characters in *The Simple Gift* make us wonder, like Herrick, "if the wrong thing is really wrong, or if it's just how people take it." In this way the aspect of society and societal values are raised which link directly to the module.

Steven Herrick has become one of Australia's most popular poets. His free verse novels have all been shortlisted in the Children's Book Council of Australia's Book of the Year Awards and *The Simple Gift* was also shortlisted for the NSW Premier's Literary Awards in 2001.

PLOT OUTLINE

Billy runs away. Billy hitches a free ride west on a freight train

Billy finds his new home in a disused train carriage in the Bendarat Rail Yard.

Billy arrives in Bendarat and goes straight to the library. He meets Irene Thompson the librarian.

Billy meets Caitlin at McDonalds. See sees him eating other diners' leftovers

Billy offers Old Bill breakfast. He is turned away.

Billy meets Old Bill, drunk, homeless, living in the railway yard.

Caitlin visits Billy in his train carriage.

He buys a ring for Caitlin, deciding not to steal it.

Billy is troubled and disappointed that Old Bill spends most of his money on alcohol.

Billy and Old Bill go to work at the local cannery.

Caitlin and Billy share a picnic lunch.

The tragedy of Old Bill's past is revealed.

Billy and Old Bill visit Caitlin's home for dinner.

Caitlin visits Billy before school but sees him with Old Bill and runs away in shock.

Billy and Caitlin make love.

Billy is confronted by the police on Main Street.

Old Bill confronts the ghosts of his past by walking past Jessie's old school.

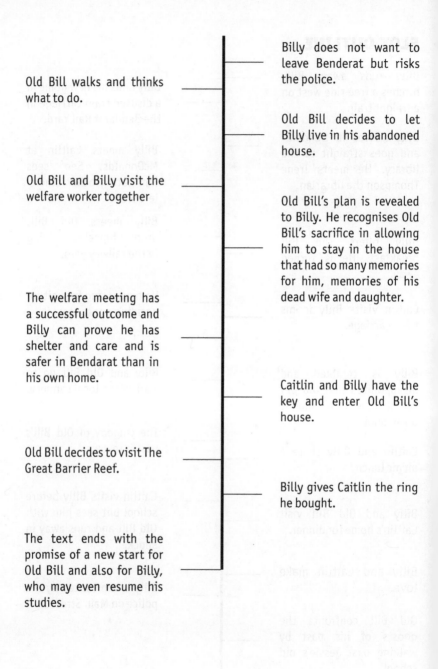

Old Bill walks and thinks what to do.

Billy does not want to leave Benderat but risks the police.

Old Bill decides to let Billy live in his abandoned house.

Old Bill and Billy visit the welfare worker together

Old Bill's plan is revealed to Billy. He recognises Old Bill's sacrifice in allowing him to stay in the house that had so many memories for him, memories of his dead wife and daughter.

The welfare meeting has a successful outcome and Billy can prove he has shelter and care and is safer in Bendarat than in his own home.

Caitlin and Billy have the key and enter Old Bill's house.

Old Bill decides to visit The Great Barrier Reef.

Billy gives Caitlin the ring he bought.

The text ends with the promise of a new start for Old Bill and also for Billy, who may even resume his studies.

ANALYSIS OF THE TEXT

Chapter One: Champagne Billy

'Champagne'

In this poem Billy describes his actions as he empties his school bag of its usual contents - books, pens, a jumper, the previous day's lunch and packs it with supplies as he prepares to run away. He packs food from the fridge as well as his father's beer, champagne and cigarettes.

The comment,

> It's the only time my schoolbag has come in handy

shows that Billy does not enjoy school. When he refers to his bag as his "travelling bag" it becomes obvious that he intends to run away.

Billy leaves a note and a bottle of lemonade on the table for his father, telling him he is "leaving home". The words,

> The old bastard will have a fit!

reveals Billy believes his father will be angry when he discovers he has left.

His attitude towards his father suggests that they share an unhappy relationship. Billy seems to gain satisfaction in the knowledge that his father would be upset to realise Billy had stolen his cigarettes and alcohol.

'Kiss the Dog'

In this poem Billy begins to describe his feelings, as well as his actions. We learn he is sixteen, and that he has nowhere to go when he leaves home:

> *I'm not proud.*
>
> *I'm sixteen and soon to be homeless.*

Notably, Billy describes the home he has been living in as a "dump" that was not even fit for the dog to live in. "Bunkbrain", Billy's dog, seems to be aware that something is wrong:

> *Bunkbrain knows something,*
>
> *he nuzzles in close,*

The closeness between the boy and his pet is evident, and highlights the lack of affection he feels towards his father:

> *I scratch behind his ears*
>
> *and kiss the soft hair*
>
> *on his head.*
>
> *I'll miss you dog.*

It is evident, however, that Billy is practical — he is aware that he will have more chance of getting a ride without the dog than with it and so leaves it behind.

'Longlands Road'

In this poem a series of images provide the responder with an impression of the street on which Billy has grown up. The broken down truck that no-one cares about fixing ("Old Basten's truck still on blocks), "grass unmown around all the doors" and "the windows in the Spencer house still broken/ from New Year's Eve," suggest that the whole street is run-down and unkempt.

Billy refers to his own violence and destructiveness in a past incident:

> Mrs Johnston's mailbox on the ground
> after I took to it with a cricket bat last week.

The responder feels sympathetic towards Billy when he refers to this place as:

> My street
>
> My suburb.

The adjectives he uses, including *"dead-beat"; "no-hoper"; "Shithole"; "lonely"* and *"downtrodden"* to describe the houses in the street indicates the resentment he feels towards this place and how negative his experience of growing up has been.

Billy interprets the noisy sound of the personified rocks hitting the roofs of the houses as a form of *"protest"* at having to remain. Such description reminds the responder of how negatively Billy feels towards this *"damn place."*

'Wentworth High School'

Billy makes one last visit to his High School before he leaves town. The mood and atmosphere of this poem is enhanced by the poet's description of the weather and the use of pathetic fallacy:

The Wind howls and the rain sheets in

Billy's reference to himself as a *"lucky bastard"* in comparison to the twenty six other students in *"Mr Cheetam's"* class who will return to *"learning/ about the geography of Japan"* suggests that he believes he is fortunate to be leaving school. Even the teacher's name suggests the students of Wentworth High School are cheated of a good education.

An antagonistic and rebellious side to Billy becomes evident. He has stolen a red lipstick from K-Mart and uses it to graffiti the classroom window. His intention is to antagonise the teacher:

Let Cheetam chew on that

'Westfield Creek'

In this poem, Billy reveals that he spent as many days at Westfield Creek as he did at school. The opening line of this poem, *"I love this place';* immediately establishes a positive tone which is enhanced through the cumulation of serene and peaceful images that are part of this natural setting. The stark contrast between this place and Billy's home and suburb is striking.

It is also significant that birds, symbols of flight and freedom, feature in this description:

> and the birds, hundreds of them,
>
> silver eyes and currawongs,
>
> kookaburras laughing

Billy's love of reading is also introduced in this poem. It becomes apparent that books have allowed Billy to transcend his experiences, at home in Longlands Road and at Westfield High. Reading has provided him with a passage into a world other than his own:

> I can read.
>
> I can dream.
>
> I know about the world.

The poem establishes an alternative to the traditional education that failed Billy:

> I learnt everything I need to know
>
> In books on the banks
>
> of Westfield Creek,
>
> my favourite classroom.

'Please'

Billy becomes increasingly desperate for a ride "west", away from his old life:

Two hours in the dark

in the rain

in the dirt of this bloody road

is not getting me anywhere.

The composer's use of repetitive structure emphasises Billy's desperation.

In addition, the responder becomes increasingly aware of Billy's reasons for running away from home and his father:

He'd be sober because I stole

his beer

his champagne.

No. I can't go back.

'Freight Train'

In this poem Billy climbs aboard an empty freight train for a free ride "west". He rides in a speedboat that is strapped to one of the carriages, although he is curious about why it is there:

A speedboat on a train

heading west?

To what?

A coalfield lake?

The inland river system

dry as a dead dingos bones?

Significantly, the escape Billy has dreamt of is made possible by this *"Aquadream speedboat."*

'Cold'

Within a very short time Billy is freezing. A metaphor is used to describe the power of the wind and rain:

> *when you've got no window to close and the wind and rain*
>
> *hits you in the face*
>
> *with the force of a father's punch.*

This provides further insight into the reality of Billy's life with his father - the reality of the world he is leaving behind.

'Keep Warm'

Billy is discovered by Ernie, the train driver, who is also the owner of the speedboat. Written from Ernie's perspective, this poem reveals his generosity and kind treatment of Billy:

> *Get your bag*
>
> *and come back to the Guard's van.*
>
> *There's a heater that works*
>
> *and some coffee.*

'Men'

Billy draws a comparison between Ernie and his own father. He lists Ernie's qualities — his friendliness, generosity and appreciation of the simple pleasures in life, implying that his own father has none of these:

> *There are men like Ernie*
>
> *and*
>
> *there are other men,*
>
> *men like my dad*

'Sport'

Written in past tense, this poem, told from Billy's perspective, is a flashback. Billy remembers breaking a bedroom window with a soccer ball, whilst playing in the backyard and most significantly, his father's aggressive reaction.

Repetition of *"I was ten years old"* emphasises the inappropriateness of his father's behaviour and reinforces the suggestion of physical abuse made earlier in the chapter.

'Another Crossing'

Back in the present tense Billy eats and drinks the sandwiches and coffee offered to him by Ernie. He leaves his father's champagne as a gift as Billy is grateful for Ernie's kindness and generosity. It is evident that Billy recognises Ernie's important role in his own passage to a new world and way of living.

CHAPTER QUESTIONS

- What does the responder learn about the character of Billy in this chapter?
- How have poetic techniques been used to introduce the responder to Billy and the world of Longlands Road?
- Explain the significance of the comparison between Ernie and Billy's father.
- How has Herrick used flashback as a narrative technique in this chapter?

CHAPTER TWO: BENDARAT

'Bendarat'

The train draws close to Bendarat early in the morning, and although Billy can see the headlights of a ute driving beside the train track, he can make out few other details because the *"dawn is fog-closed and cold"*

It is significant that Billy's exit from the train coincides with the personification of, *"..the sun finally / lifting the fog"* This is symbolic of a new beginning for Billy — a new set of experiences in a new place.

'Tonight, and the night after'

In this poem Billy draws a parallel between himself and Bendarat, where *"...every shop has a SALE sign / like the whole town's desperate for money."*

We realise that, despite his bravado (*"better a bum than a school kid"*), Billy is anxious about his uncertain future. His use of a simile to describe the *"cast-iron streetlamps / like crazy ghosts lurking/ on the footpaths"* reminds the responder that as well as hopes and dreams Billy has fears and anxieties about the life ahead of him in this *"old town / with stone buildings and wide streets"*, his new world.

Significantly, the library provides a refuge for Billy and reading a form of escapism, an opportunity to lose himself in the dreams of a safe and secure life:

My day today is reading,

reading about people who don't need money and people

who have somewhere to sleep

tonight,

and the night after.

'Lord of the lounge'

The book read by Billy in the library is an allusion to the well-known novel by William Golding called *Lord of the Flies*. Not only does Billy empathise with the characters in this story, but he uses them and their experiences to evaluate himself and his own place in the world:

I'm there on the island gorging on tropical fruit

trying to decide whose side I'm on.

Through his reading of the novel he concludes that he is outside within society, neither a rule-maker nor a rule-breaker:

...you do the only thing possible, you avoid the rules.

The librarian

Billy's inherent distrust for anyone in authority is revealed through his initial reaction to the Librarian:

Her badge says

Irene Thompson — Chief Librarian

Trouble I'm sure.

However, he seems surprised by her open friendliness, admitting *"She's OK"*. It is evident that Billy is using his past experiences to make sense of the new.

'Lunch'

Repetition of the line *"I'm poor, homeless / but I'm not stupid"* throughout this poem is significant. Billy is referring to his practical strategies for making his money last; being thrifty and frugal with food and his free entertainment, watching the couple kissing in the park.

'The Motel Bendarat'

After ruling out the park, church and railway platform as potential sleeping places, Billy discovers his new home — a disused railway carriage in the freight yard.

'Night'

Alone in the carriage at night Billy eats, sleeps and thinks — in particular about his dog Bunkbrain who he left behind. He is safe and warm, but he is lonely:

> *...I wish I had brought him*
>
> *for the company on nights like this in a new town*
>
> *and in a new home.*

'Eating Out'

Billy is matter-of-fact in his description of how he sits in McDonalds drinking lemonade and reading the paper whilst he waits to claim other diners' leftovers:

> They get up to leave
>
> and before they've reached the stairs
>
> I'm over at the table
>
> grabbing the burger and the fries
>
> to go with my lemonade,
>
> the lemonade that I bought

Billy expresses a certain satisfaction at having avoided paying for his meal (*"This is the only way to eat at McDonalds".*) His comment reflects his disdain for this multinational corporation and the kinds of values it represents:

> I order a small lemonade,
>
> no ice, no fries, no burger
>
> and no smile from the lady behind the counter...
>
> ...who looks at me as if I'm diseased for ordering only a drink.

CHAPTER QUESTIONS

- Why do you think Billy makes the library his first stop in Bendarat?
- What is the significance of the composer's allusion to *Lord of the Flies* in this chapter?

CHAPTER THREE: CAITLIN

'Caitlin and mopping'

This poem introduces the character of Caitlin, retelling the events in McDonalds from her perspective. Although Billy's behaviour confronts and challenges her:

> When I first saw what he did
>
> I wanted to go up
>
> And say
>
> 'Put that food back'
>
> But how stupid is that?

Caitlin realises the remaining food was destined for the garbage and that the hungry Billy may as well have it. Caitlin's respect for him is also evident:

> He looked self-contained,
>
> as though he knew he had to eat and this was the easiest way.

There is an immediate, although unspoken connection between the two of them:

> He stood there
>
> almost daring me to get the manager who I hate
>
> almost as much as I hate mopping.
>
> So I smiled at him.
>
> ...He sat in his chair and smiled back
>
> And I felt good.

'Too Rich'

This poem provides an insight into the character of Caitlin who, unlike Billy, has a stable family home and wealthy parents:

> *I don't need to work at McDonalds.*
>
> *Dad would rather I didn't*
>
> *He buys me anything I want.*

However, it is evident that Caitlin, like Billy, is searching for a kind of meaning that she cannot find in her world — the world of *"Discipline and Charity and Honesty"* at Bendarat Grammar School. Her home world; the values of a father, *"too rich for his own good"* with whom she feels at odds, prompts her to admit,

> *and I can't wait for university so I can leave home*
> *and that's why I work at McDonalds and mop floors.*

'Billy'

Billy is wary of Caitlin. Her clean hair, pale skin and expensive watch imply that she belongs to a world of which he has never been a part,

> *my first thought was to hate her because of that shiny watch and*
> *her perfect skin...*

However, he is surprised by her reaction to him and realises that he has underestimated her:

> *but she just smiled*
> *and complained about the mopping as if we were both caught*
> *doing something*
> *we didn't want to do but had to.*

'Breakfast'

This poem opens with a description of the simple things that make Billy happy about his new life in Bendarat:

> Bendarat is the perfect town.
>
> A friendly librarian,
>
> A warm McDonald's,
>
> Luxury train accommodation,
>
> And the town is surrounded by apple and pear orchards.

However, it is also evident that through his experiences in Bendarat, particularly his association with Caitlin, Billy is beginning to change his attitudes and values in relation to people who experience life differently from himself:

> All the students look clean
>
> and rich and smug
>
> and confident,
>
> and I thought of Caitlin
>
> and decided I shouldn't judge,
>
> not yet anyway.

This realisation marks a transition from Billy's prejudices and assumptions to a more considered approach to issues. In this way, Billy's life experiences are contributing to his maturation.

'Hunger'

It is evident that there is romance developing between Billy and Caitlin. Caitlin says:

Now I'm not going to admit

to liking the work at McDonald's, particularly mopping,

but since Billy arrived

it's certainly more interesting.

By the end of this poem Caitlin acknowledges her physical attraction to Billy whose note, which he left her to find when she cleaned his table, suggested that he had similar feelings for her.

'Manners'

Caitlin introduces herself to Billy who stands up and shakes her hand. Although there is a familiarity between them, Billy is a paradox to her as he has

Such perfect manners,

yet is found,

…eating scraps at McDonald's.

'Business'

Billy gives Caitlin a business card when he leaves the restaurant:

Billy Luckett
Unemployed Friend
Carriage 1864
Bendarat Freight Yard
No Licence/ No Certificate.

He has initiated the next stage in their relationship.

'Caitlin'

Herrick introduces Caitlin's friends Kate and Petra into the narrative in this poem, as well as Caitlin's experience with boys:

I think about boys
but only in a general way

The implication is that her feelings toward Billy constitute a new experience for Caitlin, *"a normal seventeen-year-old"* who has never felt this way about a particular boy before.

CHAPTER QUESTIONS

- What does the responder learn about the character of Caitlin from her introduction in this chapter?
- Explain why Billy is a paradox to Caitlin.
- How has Billy's earliest interaction with Caitlin begun to change how he interacts with and responds to others?

CHAPTER FOUR: THE HOBO HOUR

'The hobo hour'

The character of Old Bill is introduced into the narrative in this poem. It is evident immediately that Old Bill is both homeless and an alcoholic.

It is significant that the two meet early in the morning - symbolic of the beginning of not only their friendship, and also the dawning of important changes in both of their lives:

> *We both sit*
>
> *staring at the beer*
>
> *and the sunrise,*
>
> *sharing the hobo hour.*

'Old Bill'

Billy learns that Old Bill has been living, on and off, in the Freight Yard for several years and that it was his birthday. Billy also realises that Old Bill is not as old as his unkempt appearance suggested:

> *When you looked closer*
>
> *he wasn't that old,*
>
> *forty-five, maybe fifty.*

Our curiosity about Old Bill and the past that has led to his current circumstances is engaged almost immediately:

He got up to go to bed

to sleep off his sorrow

or so he said

It is also evident that Billy is affected by his meeting with Old Bill:

and I shivered

as the sun came up.

'Rich Town'

Billy learns from Old Bill that Bendarat was once an affluent railway town. However, improved roads and a shift from the transport of cargo by train to semitrailers meant the loss of more than one hundred jobs. It is implied that one of these jobs was Old Bill's:

and, like the few workers left,

he's got nowhere else to go

and nothing else to do,

in Bendarat

that once

was a rich town.

© Five Senses Education Pty Ltd

'Before my time'

Billy's sleep is disturbed by both the sounds of Old Bill's restless sleep and by dreams of himself in years to come, living the life of a hobo like Old Bill:

I lay in bed

listening

afraid to fall asleep

and dream again

of myself

getting old

long before my time.

'Too early'

Billy takes a bowl of Weet-Bix to Old Bill in the morning. The older man, however, is still sleeping and sends him away, unappreciative of the gesture. Billy concludes:

It was too early

for a drunk,

too early for most of us I guess.

"Too early" in this context, could be seen to have a double meaning. On a literal level, Billy is referring to the time of day – it was too early to wake him, however, it can also be interpreted as too early to reach out in friendship to Old Bill who was still a relative stranger. His reference in the final line to "the fragile morning" suggests that Billy is hurt by the rejection, that he himself is fragile.

'Bendarat River'

In this poem Billy describes an idyllic spot along the Bendarat River where every second day he washes himself and his clothes. The conclusion of the poem suggests that this is a therapeutic time for Billy who is able, for this short time, to escape his worries and fears:

> *I come here*
>
> *to the Bendarat Laundry*
>
> *to wash the world away.*

'Old Bill'

This poem introduces the voice of Old Bill. Firstly, Old Bill's low estimation of himself seen in descriptions such as, "a bum like me." He is incredulous and touched by Billy's gift of the cigarettes:

> *I almost cried,*
>
> *a kid like that*
>
> *with nothing*
>
> *giving stuff away.*

Just as 'Before my time' confronts Billy with his possible future,

> *I lay in bed/...afraid to.../dream again/of myself/getting old/ long before my time (p. 54)*

This poem raises Old Bill's past:

and I sat in my carriage

smoking

and trying to place

the past five years

And, Old Bill, like Billy is afraid of his future. Old Bill cannot face his past. His drinking and homelessness are clearly, like Billy's reading, his chosen method of escapism. A further, although brief, insight into the mystery of his past is provided through his reference to *"My darling Jessie"*.

The composer's use of figurative language in this poem is effective. Concrete images are used to describe the non tangible concept of memory:

and my memory

flickered and grew dim like the cigarette.

'Caitlin Visiting'

Caitlin explains how, with the help of her school-friend Petra, she misleads her parents in order to visit Billy in his train carriage home. Caitlin's resentment of her father, who, she admits, spoils her and buys her, *"completely stupid / unnecessary crap like / a gold watch / and a mobile phone"* stems from him treating these purchases as substitutes for really understanding his daughter. Caitlin's resentment is evident throughout this poem.

'Billy's Cave'

Caitlin describes Billy's train carriage home as:

> *...a little cave,*
>
> *a warm, safe little cave*
>
> *for children to hide in*
>
> *when*
>
> *they're scared or lonely*
>
> *and need somewhere safe*
>
> *to go.*

Caitlin recognises that his home in the Freight Yard is a refuge for Billy.

'Picnic'

When Billy realises that the knock on the door of his carriage is Caitlin, not the Police or Railway Security, his fear is replaced by nervousness. Significantly, Billy does not feel judged, but valued by Caitlin:

> *She's cool.*
>
> *She didn't sneer or*
>
> *look uncomfortable.*
>
> *She sat on the seat*
>
> *and put her feet up*
>
> *as though she belonged.*

'Happen'

In this poem Caitlin is forced to question what will or can happen in her relationship with Billy. The fact that Caitlin and Billy belong to two very different and separate worlds is most obvious.

In stark contrast to the earlier description of Billy's train carriage home is that of Caitlin's school:

> *with its stone tower*
>
> *and huge clock*
>
> *and teachers dressed in suits*
>
> *and the Indoor Sports Centre*
>
> *with its heated pool*
>
> *and the rose garden*
>
> *skirting the circular driveway...*

By listing these features of Caitlin's physical school environment the composer reminds us that when she isn't with Billy, Caitlin belongs to an established world of wealth, traditional values and high educational expectations.

Transitions in such environments might be expected to be towards tertiary education at established universities and eventually travel and marriage within the same social class.

'Going Nowhere'

Billy's feelings for Caitlin and her place in his life are described metaphorically:

a circuit of plans

with Caitlin at the centre,

and me

a badly-dressed satellite

spinning crazily in her orbit

CHAPTER QUESTIONS

- Why do you think the composer has chosen to name his two main characters Billy and Old Bill?
- Explain the initial affect of meeting each other on Billy and Old Bill.
- How has imagery been used throughout this chapter?

CHAPTER FIVE: WORK

'Sorry'

Feeling guilty about swearing at Billy for waking him too early with breakfast, Old Bill returns the favour by telling Billy about the opportunity for work at the cannery in the area. It is ironic that Old Bill finds himself:

> *looking for work*
>
> *work I don't need,*
>
> *or want.*
>
> *Walking with the kid*
>
> *early Monday morning.*

'Work'

In this poem Billy describes his work, cutting the rotten parts out of overripe tomatoes, at Golden Crest Cannery. He doesn't enjoy the work and is motivated only by the promise of a pay-check at the end of the week.

'That bloody kid'

Old Bill complains about the routine of the working week:

> *This is what I get*
>
> *for feeling sorry*

It is evident that Billy has, to some degree, assumed the role of carer for Old Bill, waking him in the morning, taking him breakfast and escorting him to work.

Old Bill's complaints about the work and about Billy are good-natured:

> *...I've half a mind to tell him*
>
> *to get her to go to work with him*
>
> *and leave me alone,*
>
> *but he prattles on*
>
> *until we reach the cannery...*

The theme of reciprocity is explored through the relationship shared by Billy and Old Bill, and is evident in this poem. Old Bill confesses that he has not worked in years and, in fact, he has not done anything much in years. Old Bill admits the job and Billy's concern for him meant he had curbed his drinking and he joked that he may even become healthy.

'My hands'

By the end of his first working week, Billy is almost sick at the thought of tomatoes:

> *at McDonalds...*
>
> *I prayed the burgers*
>
> *were without sauce*
>
> *and I couldn't eat the fries*
>
> *splashed with blood-thick liquid.*

'Burning'

Billy's pay-cheque is more money than he has ever had in his whole life. However, unlike Billy, for whom the money provides hope and possibilities, for Old Bill it is destructive. Billy is disappointed when he realises that Old Bill will drink until all of his money is gone:

> 'Drink it.,
>
> drink it probably,
>
> and piss it all away.'

'Rich'

As Billy muses over how to spend his money he begins to realise that with it comes complications — the need to worry over decisions that don't exist when you have no money at all. This poem introduces the paradox of being "rich and penniless."

'Green'

In this poem, Billy reflects on his decision not to steal the ring that he eventually bought for Caitlin. He decides against it, not only because he wants to stay in Bendarat without fear of being caught, but also because of the respect shown to him by the jeweller, who overlooked the fact that he looked "far too poor to buy anything" and spent time:

> pointing out the best ones
>
> pointing to his favourites
>
> and letting me take my time.

'Sleep'

The fact that Billy is the only person in Old Bill's life who cares for him becomes increasingly evident in this poem. Billy describes finding Old Bill, drunk and asleep, on the gravel next to the train track and taking him back to his carriage to sleep it off.

'Need'

In this poem Billy explains why he helps Old Bill "for no reason other than he needs it" It is out of recognition for the kindness of Ernie, Irene Thompson (the Librarian) and his neighbour in Longlands road who helped him.

'The mop and bucket'

Caitlin invites Billy on lunch date in this poem. This links back to the poem 'Happen' in Chapter Four - despite the differences between them, Caitlin is pursuing her relationship with Billy.

'Caitlin'

From this poem it is evident why her relationship with Billy and the possibilities it entails is so important to Caitlin. Despite being surrounded by every material thing she could ever want and need she feels incomplete:

> *And I'm not a spoilt brat OK,*
>
> *but I am spoilt,*
>
> *spoilt to boredom,*
>
> *and smart enough*

to realise that none of this

means anything...

'Lunchtime'

When Caitlin tells her girlfriends at school about her plans with Billy for the next day, her friend Kate confesses *"I had sex once."*

'Grateful'

Caitlin reiterates Kate's confession. It is a secret she has kept from her friends for a year. Sex was a negative experience that she has not been able to talk about. The uncomfortable silence amongst the three friends is juxtaposed with the closeness of the Year Nine girls who *"link arms and walk into class"* with Caitlin staring at them to avoid eye contact with her friend.

'No Hurry'

Caitlin meets Billy at the Freight Yard and they take their picnic lunch to his favourite bend in the river. The use of alliteration (*"the sun is sparkling Saturday"*) enhances the earlier description of this idyllic place.

'The Picnic'

Told from Caitlin's perspective, this poem continues the narrative of the picnic shared by Billy and Caitlin. After eating their lunch they fall asleep together in the sun. However, the physical intimacy developing between Caitlin and Billy who are *"content to waste the hours close"* is in stark contrast to the hurried physical encounter experienced by Kate (See 'Grateful').

'Truth and beauty'

In this poem, vivid imagery is used by Old Bill to describe his glass of beer:

> *the deep radiant colour*
>
> *burning gold,*
>
> *the bubbles dancing*
>
> *ballet-perfect to the rim,*

Use of descriptive words such as *"beautiful, radiant"* and *"perfect"*, contribute to the positive tone of first part of the poem, setting up the idea that a glass of cold beer constitutes *"truth and beauty"* for Old Bill. The use of sensory description in *"sweet-bitter smell of malt and barley"* add to the praise and this poem could be considered an ode.

However, the final lines of the poem reveal that this drink in fact destroys truth and beauty:

> *...downed it*
>
> *in one ignorant gulp*
>
> *and I called for another*
>
> *as all thoughts of*
>
> *truth and beauty ·*
>
> *washed from my mind.*

'Old Bill's fall'

This poem finally reveals the events in Old Bill's life that have led to his current circumstances. He explains the accident that took the life of his ten-year old daughter Jessie:

> *my sweet lovely Jessie*
>
> *fell*
>
> *and I fell with her*
>
> *and I've been falling*
>
> *ever since.*

'The house'

Old Bill continues to reveal the events of his past in this poem:

"My wife died a year to the day after Jessie." The responder learns that Old Bill still owns and visits his family home but cannot face the idea of either living there or renting or selling it to another family. It's the memories he finds here that cause him to *"get so drunk / I sleep for days. / I sleep / and / I don't dream."*

CHAPTER QUESTIONS

- Why is this first poem in this chapter called 'Sorry'?
- What does Billy mean by "rich and penniless" in the poem 'Rich'?
- In the poem 'Green', what stops Billy from stealing. the ring? What insight does this provide us into his character?
- In the poem 'Need', Billy explains why he helps Old Bill.
  a. What are his reasons?
  b. How does this make you feel?
- Reread 'Truth and Beauty'.
  a. Identify and explain the poet's use of imagery in this poem.
  b. What is significant about the use of the word 'ignorant' in the fifth last line of the poem?
- Explain the circumstances that have led to Old Bill's "hobo" lifestyle.

CHAPTER SIX: FRIENDS

'Comfort'

In this poem Billy compares his former life with his new one. He reveals that, as a student at Wentworth High, he was an outsider:

> *I never talked to girls,*
>
> *I hardly talked to anyone.*

He spent his time avoiding people not only at school, but also his father at home. By comparison, his new home *"is special"*. Billy states, *"it's mine."*

Billy also reveals his hopes for his relationship with Caitlin:

> *...I don't know*
>
> *what she sees in me.*
>
> *I hope it's*
>
> *someone to talk to*
>
> *someone to look in the eye*
>
> *knowing they'll look back.*

'Old Bill and the Ghosts'

Billy's statement that at Wentworth High he *"didn't have any friends"* in the previous poem, highlights the significance of his friendship with Old Bill:

Old Bill and me are friends.

Sometimes he comes into

my carriage and we share a beer.

Old Bill's genuine interest in Billy's daily life, the books he reads and his hopes and dreams contrasts with the disinterested and violent father Billy left behind in Longlands Road.

It is also significant that Old Bill shares the "ghosts"of his past with Billy — the memories that he can neither live with nor live without. Billy's empathy for Old Bill is evident and expressed in words such as,

And at that moment I know

I am listening to

the saddest man in the world.

'Lucky'

The growing intimacy between Caitlin and Billy is evident throughout this poem in metaphors such as,

Billy has become the diary entry

of my days.

Through the experience of her relationship with Billy, Caitlin is able to begin to make sense of herself, to define herself independently of her family and the institutions she is part of:

"and as I tell him all this

I don't feel rich or poor,

or a schoolgirl or a McDonalds worker,

or anything but lucky,

simply lucky.

'Dinner'

Caitlin's description of dinnertime in her family home reveal parental pressures about her career and tertiary education. Contrasted with these expectations and stress factors is the "simply lucky" that Caitlin finds when she is with Billy.

'The weekend off'

With the house to herself for the weekend, Caitlin's makes plans to invite Billy over. Her reference to her family home as *"this big ugly five-bedroom/million dollar brick box/that we live in"* is significant as it reveals a rejection of materialistic values.

'Hobos like us'

Billy describes his morning routine in this poem, making and sharing breakfast with Old Bill who groans and complains. He also notes the irony in the fact when Old Bill had a family to share breakfast with he was always too busy, but now that they're gone he has *"all the time in the world.'*

The positive influence of Billy over Old Bill is particularly evident. In Billy, Old Bill has found hope:

And when he does

and he dives

fully clothed into the river

his laugh becomes real

and it's a good laugh,

a deep belly roar...

'The kid'

Old Bill is aware of Billy's positive influence over him and appreciates it. His desire to reciprocate Billy's kindness is also evident:

Billy deserves more
than an old carriage
and spending his days
trying to keep an
old hobo from too much drink...

CHAPTER QUESTIONS

- What are the significant differences between Billy's former life and his new on in Bendarat?
- How does the time spent by Caitlin with her parents compare with time spent with Billy?
- What does Billy hope Caitlin "sees in" (finds attractive about) him and what does this suggest about his values?
- Reread the poems 'Dinner' and 'The Weekend Off'.
  a. What comment is the composer making about rich people and their lifestyles?
  b. Is this representation biased? Explain.
- How do we know that Billy has become as important to Old Bill as Old Bill has to him?

CHAPTER SEVEN: THE SIMPLE GIFT

'The shadows'

Caitlin visits Billy before school to tell him about her plans for the weekend, but discovers him helping Old Bill. Confronted by the scene, she runs away.

'The afternoon off'

Reflecting on her behaviour, Caitlin realises that despite always having known about the way Billy lived and survived that seeing him with Old Bill made her think of him as a hobo. She realises that she is not as free of the values and attitudes of her parents as she thought. She states,

> and maybe I was more spoilt
>
> than I thought,
>
> maybe there was something
>
> of my parents in me,
>
> whether I liked it or not ...

Determined not to give in to this she leaves school and returns to the Freight Yard.

'In the sunshine'

Sitting with Billy and drinking coffee from the same flask he shared with Old Bill, Caitlin continues to feel ashamed of her behaviour. The allusion to the well-known novel, *The Grapes of*

Wrath, by John Steinbeck, and the message about *"the honour of poverty"* that Billy finds in the text is significant. It reflects his own search for an honourable life, despite his circumstances.

'A man'

Caitlin asks both Billy and Old Bill to dinner at her house ("the thought of me/running to school/shamed me into asking".) As she talks about Old Bill, *"the saddest man in the world"* with Billy she realises that her reaction came with her immaturity and naivety about the world. Caitlin realises:

> *that Billy was sixteen years old and already a man and I was seventeen*
>
> *nearly eighteen*
>
> *and still a schoolgirl.*

'Cooking and eating'

Caitlin prepares for her "valued guests" — by cooking, getting expensive wine from her father's cellar and having a long hot bath.

'The moon'

The comparison between Billy and Old Bill's visit to "the richest house in Bendarat" with "visiting the moon" creates a metaphor for the social distance between these characters, a reminder that they belong to two very different worlds:

...Old Bill kept

wandering from room to room

discovering

another side to the moon.

'Stories'

The three eat together, on the floor in front of the open fire, not at the expensive dining room table as Caitlin and Billy share stories and anecdotes. Old Bill's pleasure in the experience is evident:

Old Bill sat quiet,

a faint smile

as he slowly drank Dad's expensive wine

and listened

to our exaggerated

stories.

'Simple gift'

Old Bill reflects on the evening as he walks home:

and I realised as I walked home

that for a few hours

I hadn't thought of anything

but how pleasant it was

to sit with these people and to talk to them.

This poem explores the value and power of friendship.

Billy stays at Caitlin's house and the young couple make love in Caitlin's bedroom. A knock on the door at 9am Monday morning happens to be Old Bill rather than Caitlin's parents!

'Monday'

This poem reveals a turning point for Old Bill, who wakes Billy (instead of the other way around) with their usual breakfast — a coffee and bowl of Weet-Bix. It is evident that this breakfast routine has become a highlight for him, as is the camaraderie between them:

> *two hobos laughing,*
>
> *laughing the morning away.*

'Tell the world'

In this poem Caitlin struggles with whether or not to tell her friends about her night with Billy. She decides not to, hardly convinced that something that seemed so perfect could be real:

> *...I wanted to prove it*
>
> *to myself*
>
> *before I tell the world.*

'Share'

Caitlin explains that sometimes, on her way to work, she takes food from her parent's home to share with Billy. He hesitates to accept this charity until Caitlin reminds him of their wealth and he resolves to share the offerings with Old Bill.

'Billy, dancing'

Billy spends the day decorating his train carriage with twenty four candles ready for Caitlin:

> *"to walk into*
>
> *the brilliant soft light*
>
> *of twenty-four candles*
>
> *dancing for her."*

'Heaven'

The union between Billy and Caitlin provides both of them with a means of escape from their reality:

> *"As I stepped into the carriage I closed the door*
>
> *to everything,"*

'The clink of the bottles'

The positive influence of Billy on Old Bill continues. In this poem he buys non-alcoholic ginger beer to share with his old friend and it is evident to the responder that Old Bill is beginning to make positive changes in his life as a direct result of his friendship with Billy:

so maybe

just maybe

I'll work on less beer

for a while.

For the kid's sake.

CHAPTER QUESTIONS

- Why is Caitlin shocked by the sight of Billy and Old Bill drinking coffee together when she makes a surprise visit before school?
- What is significant about the composer's allusion to Steinbeck's *The Grapes of Wrath?*
- Why does Herrick compare Billy and Old Bill's visit to Caitlins' house with a trip to the moon?
- Explain the development in the character of Old Bill which is evident in this chapter.

CHAPTER EIGHT: CLOSING IN

'Old Bill and his town'

The change in Old Bill, who now looks for something good in what he does everyday is most significant in this poem:

> *these people nod and say hello*
>
> *as though I'm one of them and not an old drunk.*

This contrasts with his low estimation of himself, *"a bum like me"*, early in the narrative. Old Bill is beginning to regain a purpose and meaning to his life.

'Nothing's easy'

Old Bill is actively trying to overcome his alcoholism and Billy plays an important role in helping him overcome it.

'Closing in'

Confronted by the police on the on Main Street, Billy is forced to lie about his circumstances:

> *I said I was passing through,*
>
> *I was staying with a friend,*
>
> *I'd been working in the cannery*
>
> *and now I was heading west*

However, unconvinced, the police officer leaves him with the details of a welfare officer and insists on a meeting if Billy plans to stay in town. As Billy is forced to deal with the reality of his circumstances, there is no escape for him, in his train carriage or in books as he feels the world *"closing in."*

'Old Bill's long walk'

Old Bill continues to confront his "ghosts" by walking past Jessie's school, resisting the temptation to eliminate his memories of her and the grief he still feels, by drinking. This is not easy for him but he succeeds:

I could feel my hands

shaking

as I walked back to town.

I walked the long way

careful not to go past a pub.

'Early, or late'

Billy shares his dilemma with Old Bill – to stay and risk Welfare and the Police finding out about where and how he lives or to run away, further west, leaving behind *"the only town I've ever wanted to call home / and Caitlin... "*

'Home'

Old Bill walks to think and find a solution for Billy.

'So obvious'

Old Bill's walk ends opposite his own house, where he realises,

that what I must do is

so obvious

and simple

and so unbearably painful

The implication is that he plans to share with Billy, the family home that he hasn't entered since the death of his wife.

'To help people'

Old Bill reminisces about a time when his daughter Jessie found an injured bird and nursed it back to life:

She opened her hands

and it sat on her palms

looking at her

then it turned and flew...

There is an obvious parallel here between Jessie's role in the bird's recovery and Old Bill's plan to help Billy by setting him free in the world.

'Peace'

Old Bill's description of his backyard focuses on new life the morning sun, trees in bloom, swallows nesting and *"the chirp of young birds after a feed."* After reflecting on the peace in this place, he goes about mowing the lawn and preparing it for Billy.

'The neighbours'

When questioned by the neighbours who have never seen him there before, Old Bill tells them that he is preparing the yard for *"a friend of the family"* who will be moving in soon, confirming the plan implied in earlier poems.

'War'

Caitlin can see Billy, sitting with his head in his hands in the park opposite her school, from the window of her History classroom. She can tell that something is wrong, like Billy she is trapped within her world ("I felt like /a prisoner of war/here in Room 652).

'Not moving'

Billy describes his morning in the park opposite Caitlin's school, wishing that she would come out and that they could run away together but knowing it was impossible. He can see no solution other than leaving Bendarat and is convinced that Old Bill's advice will be to do just that.

'Old Bill's suit and tie'

Before he meets with Billy to reveal his plan for the welfare meeting Old Bill buys a suit. He describes himself as *'a business man/ready to impress the world"* and the responder is keenly aware that this is exactly what he will have to do if he is going to successfully set Billy free within it.

'Near'

Having prepared to execute his plan, Old Bill rushes to meet with Billy. It is evident that he has gained as much from Billy as he intends to give him. Old Bill reflects,

> *but*
> *when I saw him*
> *I felt something*
> *I hadn't felt in*
> *many years.*
> *I felt pride.*

'All that knowledge'

In this poem we learn that Old Bill had been a white-collar worker- with an education and an office in town. But, despite this he had not been able to protect his family:

> *But all that knowledge*
> *and all that training*
> *couldn't stop a young*
> *beautiful child from*
> *falling out of a tree,*
> *or a wife from driving*
> *a car too drunk to care…*

However, it is this knowledge that empowers him with the solution he needs to help Billy, and it is being needed by Billy that makes him feel his knowledge was, *"finally worth something, finally."*

'Old and Young'

Over a cup of coffee, Old Bill reveals his plan to Billy. Recognising *"the first signs of defeat in his young eyes"* he knows he has made the right decision.

'Old Bill's plan'

Old Bill reiterates his plan and how he will present it to the Welfare:

We'll talk about

the drunken dangerous angry father.

Billy looking for work

or considering returning to school.

Welfare people like that talk.

'Billy'

Billy listens to Old Bill's plan and as he does he realises that his gift is so much more than a house to live in and an excuse for the Welfare department. Billy realises the full extent of his friend's sacrifice. He recognises the opportunity for a new life that Old Bill is making possible but at the same time fears that it will make life harder for Old Bill,

I wasn't sure

whether taking them [the keys]

meant Old Bill

had a new life too

or if taking them meant

he now had nothing,

nothing at all to hold.

'Caitlin'

Caitlin rushes out of school to find Billy but he is not there, and he isn't in his carriage home either. Worried about him she decides to return after her shift at McDonalds.

'Liars'

Billy's meeting is successful:

I don't know if Mr Stevens believed us or not,

but I knew

he couldn't do a thing about it.

I was eighteen.

I was living with a responsible adult in a normal house,

and I planned to go back to school.

All lies,

but believable lies.

Billy's change in attitude, now that he has hope, is evident. In contrast to the *"dull sunshine,"* he sat in the park, waiting in despair for Caitlin (refer to 'Not Moving'). They emerge from the office *"into bright afternoon sunshine"*. This is an example of pathetic fallacy.

CHAPTER QUESTIONS

■ Explain the techniques used by Herrick in the poem 'Old Bill and his town'.

■ What does the title 'Nothing's easy' suggest about the relationship shared by Old Bill and Billy?

■ Why does Billy feel so desperate and hopeless after being confronted by the police?

■ What is significant about Old Bill's visit to his daughter's old school ('Old Bill's long walk')?

■ What advice does Billy ask of Old Bill in the poem 'Early, or late'?

■ Explain what we learn about Old Bill in the poems 'Home', 'So obvious', 'To help people' and 'Peace'. What changes in his character do you notice from early poems?

■ Billy says "I knew Old Bill was giving me more than these keys I held. "What does he mean by this?

CHAPTER NINE: LOCK AND KEYS

'Celebrating'

Billy's relief and deep gratitude towards Old Bill is most evident:

I hugged him in Main Street

with office workers walking by, and the shopkeepers staring,

and the two old ladies at the bus stop

watching the big grey-haired man wrap his arms around the teenager.

This unprecedented display of affection between Billy and Old Bill is a clear indication of the depth of their friendship and its importance within both their lives.

It is significant that as they approach "the better part of town', Billy describes:

...swallows celebrating a birth in the nest

above the verandah.

This is a reflection of his own celebration and symbolic of his own source of new hope. Billy too has a new start and ultimately, freedom from his past, in this new world.

'Swallows'

Sitting on the verandah of Old Bill's house, Billy listens to Old Bill reminisce about his family life. The symbolism of the birds, reflecting Billy's new found hope and freedom, is sustained in this poem. Billy recognises how difficult it has been for Old Bill to offer the house to him. Despite wanting to go inside, Billy doesn't ask Old Bill. The reciprocity within their relationship is evident:

I knew better than to ask him inside.

I knew he hadn't been inside since that March day

and I wasn't going to force the issue /

not for my sake.

'Tremor'

In this poem, Old Bill recounts the afternoon on the verandah and the stories he shared. It is significant that, when shaking hands with Billy, "my hand in his / stops trembling / for a moment" Billy's positive impact on Old Bill is evident. We see that through their friendship Old Bill is given strength to overcome his drinking and then to confront the ghosts of the past that have driven him to it.

'Locks and Keys'

Billy visits Caitlin at work. He doesn't tell her about the house, but contemplates the prospect of it. We become aware that Billy is still unsure about his future, although it is evident that he will make Bendarat his home:

It's only for a short time

until...

...I can decide

what I really want to do here in Bendarat

'Caitlin and the Key'

In this poem Caitlin describes how Billy surprises her with the house. The bird motif is continued with the reference to the King Parrot in the bird feeder. Caitlin reacts emotionally to the story of Old Bill's past and the history of the house. It is also evident that she provides Billy with the support and strength he needs to pursue his future in this new world:

> *I insert the key*
>
> *and turn it slowly and push the door.*
>
> *I reach behind for Billy's hand*
>
> *and we walk inside.*

CHAPTER QUESTIONS

- How are symbolism and motif used throughout this chapter?
- "My hand in his / stops trembling / for a moment " Explain the significance of this statement by Old Bill within the context of his and Billy's friendship.

CHAPTER TEN: OLD BILL

'Old Bill'

In this poem Old Bill reflects on the advice he offered Billy early in their friendship — "to jump some freights and see the country.' He acknowledges that, by staying, Billy has changed his life and realises that he should take his own advice and take control of his life.

'A project'

This poem begins with Old Bill reminiscing about helping his daughter Jessie with a school project on The Great Barrier Reef. There is a shift in tense half-way through the poem and it is evident that The Great Barrier Reef becomes a project for Old Bill. Like Billy, we see that Old Bill is preparing to step out into the world, to escape his past and pursue his future:

I could do that

I could hop the Freights

All the way north where it's warm.

'Measure'

Billy describes the inside of Old Bill's house. Billy's observations bring Old Bill's past to life,- heightening the tragedy of his present situation. The description of the pencilled height markings on the wall is particularly poignant. Notably, the bird motif recurs in this poem, "the swallows / still sang on the verandah."

'Cleaning'

Caitlin brings supplies from her home to help Billy clean his new home. Her relationship with Billy remains a secret from her parents.

'Saturday Dinner'

In this poem Caitlin reveals that, after eating dinner with Billy for the first time in his new home, she will return to her parents and tell them about Billy and her future plans:

> I'll walk into Mum and Dad's question
>
> and I'll answer them truthfully.
>
> It's time.

'The Best Meal'

Billy recounts his afternoon with Caitlin, preparing "the best meal / I've ever eaten'. The simple pleasures he recalls, such as laughing, dancing to music, making a toast to Old Bill and sharing a meal are in stark contrast with the kind of life that Billy has left behind.

'Value'

In this poem Billy gives the emerald ring he bought with his first cannery pay to Caitlin. It is significant that this poem is called 'Value' in that it suggests the value in giving to another, as opposed to just monetary wealth. It also expresses Billy's valuing of Caitlin's love and support.

CHAPTER QUESTIONS

- Both Old Bill and Caitlin make important decisions about their futures in this chapter. What are they?
- How does Billy contribute to both Old Bill and Caitlin's ventures in a new world?

CHAPTER ELEVEN: THE HOBO SKY

'Midnight'

Unable to sleep, Billy walks back to the railway, "my home for these past few months." His silent promise not to turn his back on "the hobo life" reveals that Billy is not ashamed of how his new life has begun. It suggests that he is strengthened by it. He plans to return to the carriage once a week.

'Drinking by the River'

Descriptive language is used to describe the river setting for Billy and Old Bill's lunch meeting. This is enhanced by the use of alliteration:

> We sat by the bank
>
> watching the sun sparkle on the water
>
> with the ducks gliding by
>
> and an ibis on the opposite bank near a log
>
> looking for food,

Old Bill reveals more about his past, in particular his working life. It is significant that the ibis' search for food is juxtaposed with the mention of old Bill's Trust Account, set up during his working days — one form of survival compared with another. Transition is shown as 'Drinking by the River' connotes drunkenness, yet Bill drinks soft drink and reveals it is taking him some time to "get used to / the taste of being sober / all day".

'Respect'

Not only does this poem reflect Billy's respect for Old Bill and the home that he has loaned him, it also provides an insight into the sense of security Billy now has. He has a home in Bendarat, a "home/ where I can look out/ and not be afraid of who sees me/ or who I see."

'Maybe'

In this poem Billy tells his librarian friend Irene about his change in circumstances and he considers the possibility of continuing his education with the help of a government assistance package. Irene's concern for Billy is significant. The responder is aware that her concern for him, like that of Ernie very early in the novel, is out of the goodness of her character.

'Holiday'

Billy learns of Old Bill's plans to travel, in order to confront his "ghosts" and embrace his future. There is an unspoken understanding between them. In recalling his first meeting with Old Bill, Billy acknowledges how far he has come and how much, like Billy, his life has changed in the short time they have known each other.

'The hobo sky'

The novel ends with a new start for both Billy and Old Bill. Although they part company the union of friendship between them is ongoing:

and I looked up

into the sky,

the deep blue sky

that Old Bill and I shared

CHAPTER QUESTIONS

- Why does Billy make a silent promise not to turn his back on "the hobo life"?
- Explain how alliteration and juxtaposition are used in this chapter.

SETTING

The setting of *The Simple Gift* is significant in that changes in setting reflect Billy's movement into a new phase of his life. According to Herrick:

> *I always get a location before I get a character. I then*
>
> *put the character in the location and wait for something to happen.*

It is evident, therefore, that setting is an important technique in *The Simple Gift* and is closely linked to change and transition.

The settings associated with each character provide us with an insight into them. In addition, by showing how these characters transcend their original settings, Herrick reveals character development and transition. By leaving Longlands Road behind, for instance, Billy embarks on a journey into the world, where he discovers more about himself, others and his possibilities. In leaving Bendarat, Old Bill finally confronts his past demons and is able to move forward psychologically.

The home Billy shared with his violent, alcoholic father provides the setting for the beginning of his story and is described in the poems 'Kiss the dog' and 'Longlands Road' (Chapter One).

The negative tone of both poems is significant. Billy has no positive connections with his family home that, in his opinion, is not even fit for his dog:

> *I'd like to take him with me.*
>
> *He doesn't deserve to stay*
>
> *in this dump, no-one does.*

Herrick uses vivid descriptive language to recreate the neighbourhood of Longlands Road, from Billy's perspective:

This place has never looked

so rundown and beat

Old Basten's truck still on blocks,

the grass unmowed around the doors.

His negative attitude towards the place is most evident:

I threw one rock on the roof of each deadbeat no-hoper

shithole lonely downtrodden house

in Longlands Road, Nowheresville.

The country town of Bendarat becomes the primary setting for the text. Although a fictional place, Bendarat in its description is presented as a typical Australian country town:

It's an old town

with stone buildings and wide streets

and cast-iron street lamps

('TONIGHT, AND THE NIGHT AFTER' CHAPTER TWO).

Although once a prosperous town,"the railway hub of the south-west"(p.52), Billy recognises a sense of desperation in Benderat which seems to reflect his own circumstances. He notes,

And every shop has a SALE sign

like the whole town's desperate for money(p.21).

This is a subtle reminder of the harsh realities of life in contemporary, regional Australia.

The library provides Billy with a refuge in this new world and Carriage 1864 becomes his new home, described by Caitlin as,

> *... a little cave a warm, safe little cave for children to hide in when*
>
> *they're scared or lonely and need somewhere safe to go.*
>
> *Billy's cave.*

The contrast between Billy's "cave" and Caitlin's home,"this big ugly five-bedroom/million dollar brick box/that we live in" is most evident. Billy and Old Bill's visit to "the richest house in Bendarat" is compared with "visiting the moon" creating a metaphor for the social distance between these characters. The physical settings they belong to signify that they come from two very different worlds.

The outdoors also plays a significant role throughout *The Simple Gift* in terms of setting. This is particularly evident in 'Westfield Creek' (chapter 1), 'Bendarat River'(Chapter 4) and 'Drinking by the river' (Chapter 11). Long flowing sentences and cumulation are two techniques used by Herrick in these poems to enhance the abundance of life and natural beauty in these places.

> *I love the flow of clear water over the rocks*
>
> *and the wattles on the bank and the lizards sunbaking/ heads up/ listening/*
>
> *and the birds*
>
> *hundreds of them/*
>
> *silver-eyes and currawongs/*

> *kookaburras laughing*
>
> *at us kids swinging on the rope*
>
> *and dropping into the bracing flow. (p.6).*

In addition to the peaceful mood and positive tone of these poems, it is also significant that birds are a recurring motif, symbolic of the sense of freedom and hope Billy feels.

Finally, the poignant description of Old Bill's one-time family home features the bird motif. The house and the details of its abandonment provide an insight into the character of Old Bill, and it too becomes symbolic of the hope and freedom possible for both Billy, Caitlin and old Bill. Billy now has a home and the possibility of beginning a legitimate life in Bendarat while Old Bill has been set free from the ghosts of his past.

> *The swallows still sang on the veranda, as Caitlin and I*
>
> *stood there measuring a life (p.187).*

QUESTIONS ABOUT SETTING

- What do we learn about each of the characters by considering the settings they inhabit when they are first encountered by readers?
- How are changes in settings used to indicate movements into new phase of life?
- Explain the significance of how imagery and symbolism are used by Herrick in relation to the setting of the text and the concept of transition.

CHARACTERS

- Billy
- Old Bill
- Caitlin

Billy

Sixteen year old Billy Luckett is the main character of *The Simple Gift*. He is introduced to the reader as he runs away from his unhappy home and his abusive, alcoholic father in 'Longlands Road'. Billy's rebellious streak and his contempt for school is evident through his final visit to Wentworth High and the graffiti he leaves, in "K-mart red lipstick / stolen especially for the occasion."

Billy proves resourceful in his homelessness, buying food to eat and rationing it sensibly, finding a safe and comfortable home in an unused carriage in the Bendarat Freight Yard and eating other diners' leftovers at McDonalds. His satisfaction at avoiding paying for his meal suggests a certain disdain for McDonalds and the corporate values that this restaurant represents.

His intelligence and passion for reading and learning is also apparent. Books have allowed Billy to transcend his experiences, at home in Longlands Road and at Wentworth High. Reading and his imagination provide him with a passage into a world other-than his own:

I can read

I can dream.

I know about the world.

Significantly, Billy's first stop in Bendarat is the local library where "reading about people who don't need money / and people / who have somewhere to sleep / tonight, / and the night after," will help him escape his circumstances. It is obvious that despite his bravado, ('better a bum than a school kid), Billy is anxious about his uncertain future.

In 'Lord of the Lounge', Billy alludes to the classic novel *Lord of the Flies* and, in applying it to his own life, reveals that at this early stage in the novel, he deals with his problems by withdrawing from the world,

> *...you can't trust*
>
> *those who want to break the rules and you certainly can't trust*
>
> *those who make the rules*
>
> *so you do the only thing possible, you avoid the rules. (p.23)*

The use of first person persona and the direct nature of the verse form creates a strong sense of empathy in the responder for the character of Billy. Despite his misdemeanours, Billy is an inherently good character. He cares about people and this is most evident through his initial reaction to Old Bill ('The Hobo Hour', p.48) and their developing friendship.

In addition, the relationship and growing intimacy between Billy and Caitlin highlights the lack of such in his former life, where he "never talked to girls", he didn't have any friends" and spent his time avoiding his father. The desire to change and to be understood is revealed by Billy:

I don't know

what she sees in me.

I hope it's

someone to talk to

someone to look in the eye

knowing they'll look back.

Old Bill

Old Bill is a drunk. The Bendarat Freight Yard has been his home for the past five years. As the novel progresses Old Bill's past is gradually revealed to the responder and it becomes evident that like Billy, Old Bill has turned to the "hobo life' in order to escape his circumstances.

Unable to cope with the death of his daughter who fell from a tree in the backyard, and one year later, the death of his wife in a drink-driving accident,Old Bill turned to alcohol. He turned his back on his former, respectable, suburban life and abandoned his home, turning to alcohol to help him escape his painful memories:

I lifted the glass and downed it

in one ignorant gulp and I called for another

as all thoughts of truth and beauty

washed from my mind. (p.95)

His friendship with Billy becomes the catalyst for Old Bill to regain control of his life. Touched by Billy's initial kindness to him, ('I almost cried / a kid like that / with nothing / giving stuff away.") Old Bill tells him about casual work available at the local cannery and finds himself, although reluctantly, starting work there with Billy. Old Bill begins to drink and smoke less and to gradually confront his past and consider his future.

Ultimately, through using his education and knowledge to save Billy and to give himself the new start he needed, Old Bill regains a sense of pride, acknowledging, in his helping of Billy,

so all that knowledge

was finally worth something, finally. (p.162)

It is the knowledge that he can help Billy that gives old Bill the strength to reclaim his own place in the world:

I could do that

I could hop the freights

All the way north

Where it's warm.

I could stay there for the winter

And I could be sure

That Billy was looking after everything I own/ For when I get back

From taking Jessie's

Trip to the ocean. (p.185)

Thus, Old Bill's initial transition is due to grief, a reaction to loss and family tragedy. It is marked by loss. His second transition is a positive one. It is due to friendship and selflessness which, in turn, helps to transform his thinking and re-establish his self-confidence.

Caitlin

Seventeen-year old Caitlin's introduction into the novel coincides with her first meeting Billy. They meet in McDonalds where she works and where she sees him helping himself to leftovers for dinner.

Billy, and the reader, are aware from the outset that he and Caitlin are opposites in terms of their family background, upbringing and lifestyles. Unlike Billy, Caitlin has rich and indulgent parents, attends an exclusive private school and has plans to pursue a university education. It is evident that her earliest acknowledgement of Billy challenges the values of the world she belongs to the world of "Discipline and Charity and Honesty" at Bendarat Grammar School. Ironically, in turning against her past she is able to truly offer charity to others and be honest with herself.

Her friendship with Billy also challenges the social expectations of her parents, particularly her father, who is described as "too rich for his own good', and with whom she feels at odds.

Significantly, Caitlin is well-aware of her own privilege:

I'm not a spoilt brat OK, but I am spoilt,

spoilt to boredom,

Despite being surrounded by everything that money can buy she feels resentful towards and misunderstood by her parents. She is desperate for her independence from them:

...I can't wait for university so I can leave home

and that's why I work at McDonald's and mop floors. (p.37)

Through her relationship with Billy, Caitlin learns more about herself. This is particularly evident when she reacted to seeing Billy and Old Bill together by running away. It is with shock and surprise she recognised Billy looked like a hobo. ('The Shadows', Chapter Seven) The self-analysis that followed revealed the impact of her upbringing:

> *maybe I was more spoilt*
>
> *than I thought,*
>
> *maybe there was something of my parents in me,*
>
> *whether I liked it or not (p.117)*

Caitlin is forced to confront and to re-evaluate her own system of beliefs in order to assert her independence. Her on-going relationship with Billy provides her with an opportunity to explore and eventually find her own place in the world. Her explorations lead her to a place some distance away from the carefully regulated world valued by her parents and her school. Her different values become a catalyst for a new set of experiences which both excite and confront Caitlin and lead her towards maturity. Despite his troubled past, she decides,

> *I love Billy and I'm sure of him. I want my parents to know.*
>
> *In two weeks I'll be eighteen*
>
> *and I want my parents to know what I do,*
>
> *what I plan to do. (p.190)*

THEMES LINKED TO TRANSITION

Relationships and Change

Relationships can be seen as a theme and as a trigger for personal transition:

The Simple Gift shows how new experiences and relationships lead to growth and change for the characters of Billy, Caitlin and Old Bill. Consequently, such changes lead to new directions in their lives.

By running away from the oppression of his abusive home life and Westfield High School failure, Billy initiates a series of new experiences in his life. Ultimately, he finds freedom and independence in Bendarat, becoming self-sufficient with his job at the cannery and creating a safe and comfortable home in the unused railway carriage:

> *living in this carriage is special it's mine*
>
> *and I keep it clean*
>
> *and I read to give myself an education*
>
> *that Westfield High*
>
> *never could. (p.102)*

However, most significantly, in Bendarat Billy forms meaningful relationships. The developing intimacy between Billy and Caitlin is unprecedented for him. Through the use of metaphor in the poem 'Going Nowhere' (chapter 4) Herrick reveals how Caitlin becomes the centre of Billy's existence in Bendarat, as his life becomes:

a circuit of plans

with Caitlin at the center and me

a badly dressed satellite

spinning crazily in her orbit (p.70)

The overwhelmingly positive change this constitutes for Billy is most evident in the poem 'Comfort' (Chapter Six) in which he compares the loneliness and isolation of his old life with his new set of experiences.

Similarly, Caitlin discovers more about herself through her relationship with Billy. Through Billy's circumstances, his friendship with Old Bill and his "hobo" existence she is confronted by a world of experiences outside her own privileged lifestyle. This is most evident from her first meeting with Billy, in McDonalds:

When I first saw what he did

I wanted to go up and say,

'put that food back. '

But how stupid is that? (p.34).

Ultimately, Caitlin is challenged to re-evaluate her own system of beliefs and values and to eventually, assert her independence from her parents. Her commitment to reveal to them the truth about her relationship with Billy is indicative of her growing maturity.

In addition, the friendship between Billy and Old Bill proves to be the catalyst for a new direction in both of their lives. It is evident that Old Bill benefits from the positive influence of Billy, whose persistence and encouragement enables him to gradually regain control of his life and overcome his reliance on alcohol:

'Nothing's easy.'

That's what Billy said

When I told him about my walks and how I pass a pub

and my hand starts shaking (p.142).

Simultaneously, through the companionship and advice Old Bill provides and the mutual respect and trust that they develop for one another, Old Bill becomes a father-figure to Billy whose experience of family has only ever been dysfunctional.

The extent to which his friendship with Old Bill changes Billy's life is revealed through the climax of the story when Billy is confronted by the police. Feeling threatened by the Welfare department, he becomes miserable and is convinced that his only alternative is to run:

...it seemed that moving out west

was the only answer. But how could I leave the only town

I've wanted to call home, And Caitlin...

However, with the help of Old Bill, Billy discovers that he no longer has to "avoid the rules" (p.23) in order to survive. Rather, he is able to begin his life in Bendarat legitimately, with the security of a real home. For Old Bill, this becomes an opportunity for him to regain some pride in himself, to acknowledge the security in his past and the possibilities in his future.

Relationships in closer focus:

The Simple Gift challenges readers to think about the importance and value of relationships. Throughout the narrative, a number of significant relationships are developed and through each of these the composer explores particular ideas.

Firstly, the dysfunctional and destructive relationship shared by Billy and his father and the failure of Caitlin's parents to really understand her raises the question of what children really need from their parents. The juxtaposition of these relationships highlights that parents need to do more than just provide for their children:

> *And I know what I really need and it's not in my bedroom.*
>
> *And it's not able to be bought*
>
> *in any damn store. (Caitlin, p.88)*

The growing intimacy between Caitlin and Billy draws attention to the power of love to challenge and change ideas about others and the world. Billy begins to relate to and think differently about others through his association with Caitlin:

> *All the students look clean and rich and smug*
>
> *and confident,*
>
> *and I thought of Caitlin*
>
> *and I decided I wouldn't judge, not yet anyway.*
>
> ('BREAKFAST', P.30)

Similarly, in accepting Billy and his friend Old Bill into her life, Caitlin is forced to examine her own values and to assert her independence from her parents. She concludes,

I love Billy and I'm sure of him. I want my parents to know.

Perhaps most significant of all is the deep and touching friendship shared by Billy and Old Bill. Steven Herrick says:

I'm interested in showing how positive young people are. I want to show how young people influence older people as well as vice versa. I always like to show in my books that kind of play-off between who's influencing who.

Billy's positive influence over Old Bill is considerable. It is with Billy's help, support and encouragement that Old Bill begins to overcome his alcoholism and regain control of his life. His character development is particularly evident through a comparison of his reluctance and frustration in 'That Bloody Kid' (Chapter Five) with his changed attitude in...

I'll work on less beer for a while.

For the kid's sake. (p.137)

Significantly, the notion of reciprocity is explored through this relationship. It shows that the true essence and reward of friendship is in doing things for each other. Ultimately, it is by reciprocating Billy's kindness - with a plan that allows Billy to circumvent harsh treatment from the authorities and begin life in a real home in Bendarat that Old Bill is able to regain the self-worth and sense of pride he lost.

On another level, the text also explores the importance of the kindness of strangers, and how the expression of good will from Ernie, Irene and Billy's one-time neighbour in Longlands Road empower him. It is the capacity in these people for unconditional generosity that restores and maintains Billy's faith in people so that, despite his own hardships, he continues to value others. In the poem 'Need', he explains:

And that is why I help Old Bill, for no reason

other than he needs it

Other themes such as grief, dysfunctional families and identity could be explored in relation to exploring transitions.

Apart from themes reflecting transitions, do not forgot to explore the fact that the style of the text, a "verse novel" crosses boundaries and explores transitions relating to genre categorisation.

STYLE

Language

The verse form of *The Simple Gift* is one of its most striking features. The economy of words allowed by this form provides the linear rather than episodic narrative with momentum, an advantage noted by Herrick, who says:

> *The reader can see themselves progressing with the story. They see my stories less as poetry and more as a narrative.*

Notably, the use of alternating first person persona in the verse form contributes to an overall sense of intimacy between the characters and the responder. According to Herrick:

> *verse novels...allow one person's voice to speak directly to the reader, or to the characters. The dialogue can be more dynamic, but it can also be more intimate.*

The resulting empathy between the reader and these characters is significant in that it is through this personal connection that Herrick explores the values of his characters as they are confronted with new experiences and make their way into the world. In this way he indirectly challenges the responder to question themselves and their own values and beliefs. Not only does the reader observe Billy reading in order to gain insight, for instance, but he shares his new found insights directly with the responder. Consequently, we become aware of the power of our own reading, and therefore, of *The Simple Gift*, to challenge our ideas about our place in the world and our own ability to transition.

In addition, changing focalisation, revealing shifts between the perspectives of the three central characters, enhances the responders' engagement with them. By having each character present and reflect on the same event Herrick effectively creates authentic and complex characters and portrays dynamic interactions between them. Moreover, this aspect of the narrative style introduces depth and tension to the narrative. For instance, the responder is well aware of Old Bill's tragic past and personal struggle before he shares it with Billy. Similarly, the responder relates differently to Caitlin as a result of directly sharing her reflections on her privileged lifestyle and the wealth of her family.

Another significant aspect of the language of the text is the use of descriptive and figurative language. Vivid descriptive language is used to recreate the various settings throughout the text, including Longlands Road, Bendarat, the railway yard and, in particular, the various riverside havens in which Billy seeks refuge. Long flowing sentences and cumulation feature in such poems as 'Westfield Creek' (chap.1), 'Bendarat River' (chap.4) and 'Drinking by the river' (chap.11). Descriptions of the natural beauty and abundance of life in these places, and particularly the freedom of spirit Billy experiences there contrast with the confinement and negativity experienced in Longlands Road and at Westfield High.

Through the use of figurative language Herrick creates powerful images with an economy of language which seems to increase their intensity. This is most evident in the metaphor Billy uses to express how Caitlin and the growing intimacy between them has impacted his life:

a circuit of plans

with Caitlin at the centre,

and me

a badly dressed satellite

spinning crazily in her orbit (p.70)

This is just one example of how Herrick uses concrete images to represent the abstract feelings and emotional experiences of his characters.

In addition, shifts in tone throughout the text are indicative of the characters' changing attitudes and their changing place within the world. For instance, the negative tone of the early poems narrated by Billy, such as 'Longlands Road' and 'Wentworth High School' (Chapter One) contrasts with the positive, even optimistic tone of the poems of the later chapters, particularly the closing poem, 'The Hobo Sky'.

ESSAY QUESTION

Read the question below carefully and then examine the essay outline on the following pages. Try to develop your essay along these lines.

Also, develop strategies to answer questions that are not essay based. A list of these response types is given at the end of the sample essay. Look at these. You should be familiar with most of them. Try to practise them when you can and develop your writing skills.

QUESTION

It would be impossible to experience transitions without the help of others.

To what extent is this reflected through the texts you have studied?

In your response refer to your prescribed text and at least one other related text of your own choosing.

THE ESSAY

The essay has been the subject of numerous texts and you should have the basic form well in hand. A point to emphasise is to link the paragraphs both to each other and back to your argument (which should directly respond to the question). Of course, ensure your argument is logical and sustained.

Make sure you use specific examples and that your quotes are accurate. To ensure that you respond to the question make sure you plan carefully and are sure what relevant point each paragraph is making. It is solid technique to actually 'tie up' each point by explicitly coming back to the question.

When composing an essay the basic conventions of the form are:

> ▪ Introduction -State your argument, outline the points to be addressed and perhaps have a brief definition.

A solid structure for each paragraph is:

▪ Main Body-Topic sentence (the main idea and its link to the previous paragraph/argument)
▪ Explanation - discussion of the point including links between texts if applicable.
▪ Detailed evidence (Close textual reference-quotes, incidents and techniques discussion.)
▪ Tie up by restating the point's relevance to argument / question

▪ Conclusion -Summary of points
▪ Final sentence that restates your argument

As well as this basic structure you will need to focus on:

Audience – For the essay the audience must be considered formal unless specifically stated otherwise. Therefore, your language should reflect the audience. This gives you the opportunity to use the jargon and vocabulary that you have learnt in English. For the audience ensure your introduction is clear and has impact. Avoid slang or colloquial language including contractions (like doesn't, e.g., etc.) in essays.

Purpose – The purpose of the essay is to answer the question given. The examiner evaluates how well you can make an argument and understand the module's issues and its text(s). An essay is solidly structured so its composer can analyse ideas. This is where you earn marks. It does not retell the story or state the obvious.

Communication – Take a few minutes to plan the essay. If you rush into your answer it is almost certain you will not make the most of the brief 40 minutes to show all you know about the question. More likely you will include irrelevant details that do not gain you marks but waste your precious time. Remember, an essay is formal so do not do the following: story-tell, list and number points, misquote, use slang or colloquial language, be vague, use non sentences or fail to address the question.

ESSAY - *THE SIMPLE GIFT*

A few notes about the question:

Carefully consider what the question is actually asking you and how you can apply what you have learned about both the ideas and the language of Herrick's poetry.

Take care to meet the specific requirements of the task, particularly the number of texts the examiner asks for. There is no value in writing on more and you will definitely be penalised for writing on fewer texts.

You MUST have quotations and textual references that show you have a good knowledge and understanding of the texts you are focusing on in your answer.

Your response must look at both WHAT the texts are about (meanings) as well as HOW the composer has used textual features and language techniques to represent these ideas.

PLAN: Don't even think about starting without one!

Introduce...

The texts you will discuss in this response. *The Simple Gift* and *Good Will Hunting*

Definition:

Moving into the world involves growth and change in the individual as a result of new experiences and particularly new relationships.

Argument

Relationships become the catalyst for a character's growth in understanding of themselves and their world and provides the opportunity for the individual to take control of the direction of their lives.

You need to let the marker know what texts you are discussing. It is good to start with your definition but it could have come in the first paragraph of the body. You

MUST state your argument in response to the question and the points you will cover. Don't wait until the end of the response to reveal your ideas!

Explain how both ideas one and two above are reflected through:

a. The prescribed text - *The Simple Gift*

b. The related text - *Good Will Hunting*

Idea 1 - Relationships allow individuals to learn about themselves and their world

Idea 2- Relationships become the catalyst for individuals to take new directions in their lives and control their futures.

Adapt what you have learned about the set texts to your argument throughout the body of the essay. Provide examples for each point you make. Discuss one or two pieces of related material depending on what is asked for in the question.

- Summary of the points made about both texts.
- Final sentence that restates your argument

Make sure your conclusion restates your argument. It does not have to be too long.

ESSAY RESPONSE

"Exploring Transitions" involves considering that which motivates growth and results in change in an individual. Often such motivations are a result of new experiences and new relationships. They can be positive or negative. In Steven Herrick's verse novel, *The Simple Gift* and the film *Good Will Hunting*, directed by Gus Van Sant, the central characters experience relationships which become the catalyst for their growth in understanding of themselves and their world. Ultimately, it is through their dealings with significant others that these characters are able to take control of their lives and change the direction of their futures.

Perhaps the most significant difference between Billy's experiences living in Longlands Road and attending Westfield High where "I never talked to girls / I hardly talked to anyone" and the new life he begins in Bendarat is the meaningful relationships he forms. The overwhelmingly positive change this constitutes for Billy is most evident in the poem 'Comfort' (chapter six, p.102) in which he juxtaposes the loneliness and isolation of his former life with his new set of experiences. Through the use of metaphor Herrick reveals how Caitlin becomes the centre of Billy's existence in Bendarat, as his life becomes,

a circuit of plans

with Caitlin at the centre, and me

a badly dressed satellite—

spinning crazily in her orbit (p.70)

It is also significant that Billy begins to relate to and think differently about others through his association with Caitlin. This is particularly evident through his reaction to the students who he thought initially looked "rich and smug/ and confident' until:

> *I thought of Caitlin*
>
> *and decided I wouldn't judge,*
>
> *not yet anyway.*
>
> **(BREAKFAST, P.30)**

In addition, the friendship between Billy and Old Bill proves to be the catalyst for a new direction in both of their lives. It is evident that Old Bill benefits from the positive influence of Billy, whose persistence and encouragement enables him to gradually regain control of his life and overcome his reliance on alcohol:

> *'Nothing's easy.'*
>
> *That's what Billy said*
>
> *When I told him about my walks and how I pass a pub*
>
> *and my hand starts shaking (p.142)*

Simultaneously, through the companionship and advice Old Bill provides and the mutual respect and trust that they develop for one another Old Bill becomes a father-figure to Billy whose experience of family has only ever been dysfunctional.

The extent to which his friendship with Old Bill changes Billy's life is revealed in the climax of the story when Billy is confronted by the police and, feeling threatened by the Welfare department, becomes miserable and separate, convinced that his only alternative is to run. Billy concluded,

...it seemed that

moving out west—

was the only answer. But how could I leave the only town

I've wanted to call home,

And Caitlin...

However, with the help of Old Bill, Billy discovers that he no longer has to "avoid the rules"(p.23) in order to survive. Rather, he is able to begin his life in Bendarat legitimately, with the security of a real home. For Old Bill, this becomes an opportunity to regain some pride in himself, to acknowledge the good in his past and the possibilities in his future.

Like the relationship between Billy and Old Bill, in *Good Will Hunting* the relationship that develops between Will and Sean becomes the catalyst for a new direction in both of their lives. The opening sequence of *Good Will Hunting* introduces the main character Will in paradoxical terms - his photographic memory and mathematical genius is foregrounded in the opening montage, however, it seems at odds with his menial job as a janitor and the drinking and street brawling he engages in with his friends.

Long shots of Will alone on the train commuting to and from work and the use of blue light suggest that he is isolated and dissatisfied with his life.

Faced with a jail sentence for aggravated assault, Will is forced to participate in counselling sessions with Sean. Through these sessions Will not only begins to develop respect and trust for someone outside his immediate circle of childhood friends, he begins to understand himself, eventually understanding that the abuse he suffered at the hands of his stepfather was not his fault. He finally acknowledges the responsibilities entailed in his ability as a mathematician. Significantly, it is his friend Chuckie who helps him overcome his internal struggle between loyalty to his childhood friends and the pursuit of a life outside of the world he has always known:

> *You don't owe it to yourself, you owe it to me...it will be an insult to us if you're still here in twenty years time...hanging around here is a waste of your time.*

By the end of the film the viewer is aware that Will will not only be able to fulfil his potential as a mathematician, but will also engage in a loving and successful relationship with Skylar who he was previously unable to allow himself to trust. This is represented visually throughout the closing sequence as the camera zooms out to an extreme long-shot showing Will driving along a winding road into the distance and out of the frame.

Significantly, the notion of reciprocity in relationships leading to transitions is explored through both of these texts. *The Simple Gift* shows that the true essence and reward of friendship is in doing things for each other. Ultimately, it is by reciprocating Billy's kindness with a plan that allows Billy to avoid the authorities and begin life in a real home in Bendarat and, Old Bill is able to regain self-worth and lost pride. In *Good Will Hunting*, Sean is forced to confront the reality of his own withdrawal from life since the death of his wife through his personal connection as counsellor to Will.

Both *The Simple Gift* and *Good Will Hunting* reveal that individuals transition to better places, mentally and physically, through the help of others. Both texts present relationships as the catalysts for growth and change, as seen in their central characters, Billy and Will respectively. These relationships not only provide the characters with the opportunity for self-understanding and growth, but empower them to take a new direction and to have some control over their futures.

Now, retype this using more textual references to your core text, more analysis of poetic/narrative techniques and incorporate material on a related text of your choice rather than *Good Will Hunting*.

OTHER TYPES OF RESPONSES

It is crucial students realise that their response in the examination, class and assessment tasks may NOT always be in the form of an essay. This page is designed to give guidance with the different types of responses required.

The response types covered in the exam may include some of the following:

- Writing in a role
- Letter/ emails
- Journal/Diary Entry
- Feature Article
- Dialogue
- Speech
- Point of view
- Report
- Interview
- Essay

Students should familiarise themselves with these types of responses. You should practise each one at some stage of your HSC year.

ANNOTATED RELATED MATERIAL

In exploring transitions, students are urged to explore the genre of the Bildungsroman, as growth and development, which characterises the genre, can be linked to context, society and personal transition.

Whatever related texts you select, ensure you can discuss the transitions and how composers reveal these through use of techniques. Analyse the growth, change and consequences for individuals in these related text choices. Do characters come to new understandings, new knowledge or new perceptions about themselves, others, relationships and society?

(BOS English Stage 6 Prescriptions 2015-2019)

Text Type One: Novels

Looking for Alibrandi **Melina Marchetta**
Penguin
1992
ISBN 0 14 036046 8

Josephine Alibrandi is a girl of Italian Australian background in her last year of school. She is a scholarship girl at an exclusive school and feels out of step with most of the other students whom she sees as having perfect lives due to their money and position.

Josephine feels constrained by her Italian family and longs for her 'emancipation' from them. Over the course of the year, she has experiences which shape her. She meets her father and develops a relationship with him, she has a relationship with a boy from the local high school and she loses a friend to suicide. All of these experiences help her to forge a stronger identity. She realises that money and position are no guarantee of a perfect life and that she is in charge of her own destiny.

A Christmas Carol **Charles Dickens**

A Christmas Carol is a classic Victorian tale, set in England and written by Charles Dickens. It tells of Ebenezer Scrooge and his transformation of heart after supernatural visits. Scrooge becomes a more generous hearted person and less miserly and negative after his experiences.

The Cay **Theodore Taylor**

Puffin
1969

Set during World War One, this novel relates the difficult experiences of a young boy, Phillip Enright. Phillip's parents are presented as less than ideal. En route to England, The ship Phillip and his mother have taken passage on, is torpedoed. Phillip finds himself first of all on a raft, and then on a small island with a black man, Timothy. Phillip loses his sight as the result of an injury during the sinking of the ship.

Timothy teaches Phillip to be independent, changing him greatly. Later, Timothy protects Phillip during a hurricane, but is injured and dies. The skills which Timothy has taught him, allow Phillip to survive on his own on the island. When he is rescued, and returns to civilisation, Phillip continues to be responsible and independent. This is presented by the author as a positive development, and one which will help Phillip to grow up well.

Text Type Two : Film

Stand By Me
Directed by Rob Reiner

1986

Four friends, all twelve years old and in their last year of elementary (primary) school embark on a journey to view the body of a boy killed by a train. Although the journey is exciting and at times difficult, its main value for two of the boys, Chris and Gordie, is in the sharing of their worries and fears. Chris feels limited by his family's (justified) bad reputation. Gordie has become 'the invisible boy' in his family since the death of his brother and feels that nothing he does is valued by them. The support they offer to each other gives each a boost in confidence and they return from the journey, ready to go into the new world of high school and to take advantage of every opportunity.

Dead Poets' Society
Directed by Peter Weir

1989

In this film about growing up, a charismatic teacher, John Keating, challenges his class of teenage boys to "seize the day" and to follow their dreams. This has catastrophic results in the case of one boy, Neil, who is thwarted by his father from following his dream of being an actor and suicides. This ultimately costs Keating his job. But, his passion for life has a profound effect on many of the other boys, in particular, Neil's room-mate, Todd. Todd suffers from crippling shyness which prevents him from making use of his creative talents. A key scene of the film shows Keating covering Todd's head so that he does not have to face the other boys and encouraging him to create a poetic monologue on the spot. What Todd says is very good and reveals how talented he really is. It is implied, by the end of the film that he will go into the world with optimism and greater confidence in himself, making use of his talents.

OTHER RELATED MATERIAL

Animal Farm - Novel. George Orwell.

Beauty and the Geek - TV series. This is interesting and much could be explored regarding context and values. Whereas *Educating Rita* and *My Fair Lady*, based on *Pygmalion* (see myth and GB Shaw's play) all have male mentors and the transformation occurs to a female protagonist, the transition in this modern show occurs to male subjects. https://au.tv.yahoo.com/beauty-and-the-geek-australia/#page1

Bend It Like Beckham. Directed by Gurinder Chadra. 2002. Film. A young British Indian girl succeeds in playing soccer against the wishes of her conservative family and eventually wins a sports scholarship in America.

Butterfly. John Tranter. Poem. In this poem a young woman keeps moving into new situations or new worlds, seeking something elusive.

Cinema Paradiso. Directed by Guiseppe Tornatore. 1989. Film. A young boy, Toto's, passage to manhood. Alfredo, the projectionist at the theatre is an important mentor to him.

Dr Jekyll and Mr Hyde Stevenson, R. L. Novel

Jane Eyre -Charlotte Bronte. Novel. This book traces a young girl's life from orphaned youngster to independent adult. Her independent spirit often conflicts with societal expectations.

Legally Blonde. Directed by Robert Luketic. 2001. Film. Elle goes to college to win her boyfriend back. The film includes themes of self-actualisation and identity.

Mao's Last Dancer. Li Cunxin. Penguin, 2003. A young boy moves beyond an impoverished background to international success through ballet school. This novel is recommended highly as it strongly conveys personal and cultural transition. It can also be found in filmic and picture book forms.

My Fair Lady. Cukor, 1964. Film. This film, A musical, has close parallels to the transition of Rita in *Educating Rita*. Both texts reveal the transformation of a young woman from a lower socio-economic status. In both cases, they have male mentors to thank for educating them. A key difference, reflecting modern values, is the fact that Eliza's is an experiment whereas Rita seeks to be transformed through education.

Orlando. Virginia Woolf. Novel and Film. A classic which explores gender and sexual and historical transitions.

Pretty Woman 1990, G Marshall. Film. Vivian Ward has the opportunity to start over again, due to a chance meeting. A romantic comedy.

Romulus my Father. Raimond Gaita. Film and Memoir. A story which reveals the hardships of the migrant experience and the transition effected through a move to a new country.

The Hand Maid's Tale – Margaret Atwood. This setting is significant as it involves dystopic, societal transition. The female protagonist's identity is subject to a forced transition where she is acknowledged only in relation to a male social hierarchy.

The Road From Coorain. Jill Ker Conway. A memoir of Conway's journey from girlhood on an isolated sheep-farm in of Australia to her departure for America (and eventually the presidency of Smith College).

The Arrival. Shaun Tan. Lothian, 2006. Picture book. This visually depicts the difficulties and fears immigrants must overcome upon their arrival in a new country.

The Picture of Dorian Gray by Oscar Wilde. Novel/ Film. Dorian Gray sells his soul and the result is ageless beauty. While the portrait of Dorian transforms, his appearance does not. Until...

Zlata's Diary. Zlata Filipovic. A twelve year old records the transition and transformation that war brings to her world.

Additional Films:

- *Amelie*
- *Circle of Friends*
- *Forest Gump*
- *Freedom Writers (2007)*
- *Life is Beautiful*
- *The Matrix*

Picture Books:

Window by Jeanie Baker.

My Place by Nadia Wheatley and Donna Rawlins